AMERICAN ASTRONOMERS

Collective Biographies

AMERICAN ASTRONOMERS

Searchers and Wonderers

Carole Ann Camp

ENSLOW PUBLISHERS, INC.

44 Fadem Road	P.O. Box 38
Box 699	Aldershot
Springfield, N.J. 07081	Hants GU12 6BP
U.S.A.	U.K.

To Charles, Morgan, and Heather

Library of Congress Cataloging-in-Publication Data

Camp, Carole Ann.
    American astronomers: searchers and wonderers / Carole Ann Camp.
        p. cm. — (Collective biographies)
    Includes bibliographical references and index.
    Summary: Brief biographies of ten American astronomers, including Maria
Mitchell, Percival Lowell, and Carl Sagan.
    ISBN 0-89490-631-3   *12/97 1943 0825*
    1. Astronomers—Biography—United States—Juvenile literature. 2. Women
astronomers—Biography—United States—Juvenile literature. [1. Astronomers]
I. Title. II. Series.
QB35.C36 1995
520'.92'273—dc20   95-14472
[B]   CIP
                                  AC
Printed in the U.S.A.

10 9 8 7 6 5 4 3 2

Illustration Credits:
American Institute of Physics, p. 52; California Institute of Technology
Archives, p. 50; Courtesy of Carl Sagan, p. 84; Courtesy of Carl Sagan,
photo by Bill Ray, p. 90; Courtesy of Vera Rubin, p. 81; Courtesy of Vera
Rubin, photo by Mark Godfrey, p. 76; Hale Observatories, courtesy AIP
Emilio Segre Visual Archives, pp. 44, 60; Harvard College Observatory, pp.
28, 32, 41, 57, 68, 74; Historical Society of Delaware, p. 36; Lowell
Observatory, pp. 20, 26; Maria Mitchell Association, p. 17; Palomar
Observatory, courtesy AIP Emilio Segre Visual Archives, p. 66; Sophia
Smith Collection, Smith College, p. 12.

Cover Illustration: Courtesy of Carl Sagan, photo by Bill Ray

Contents

Acknowledgements

The author acknowledges the help of many people for their love and support, especially Susan Boone who made many trips to the library and located all of the pictures for this book.

Preface

Since the beginning of time, human beings have been curious about the sun, the moon, and the stars. Ancient peoples thought the sun and the moon were gods. Great stories and myths were created to explain why the stars were arranged in the sky the way they were. The people recognized patterns in the sky. The constellations were named, and stories were told around the world. The people noticed that some of the "stars" (the planets) did not stay in their patterns but had their own regular motion around the sky. The planets were named and stories were told. Human beings built great structures to predict the motions of these heavenly objects, from the great astronomical clock of Stonehenge on the Salisbury Plain in southern England to the Big Horn Medicine Wheel in Wyoming.

During the last hundred years, what we have learned about the sky has expanded beyond our wildest imagination. The driving force in science, and particularly in astronomy, is this intense curiosity to find out more. Even if our bodies are Earthbound, our minds and imaginations are not. The ancient astronomers were very careful observers. Night after night, people watched the sky and recorded their observations in some way, like on the ceiling of the Temple of Hathor in Egypt or on the walls of caves in Arizona. Modern astronomers are also very careful observers and recorders of these observations.

Night after night, astronomers, ancient and modern, looked to the skies searching and wondering, wondering and searching. The stories of the people in this book are stories of people who spent night after night looking at the skies searching and wondering, wondering and searching. Maria Mitchell, the first American woman professor of astronomy, made the first discovery of a comet through a telescope. She knew the sky so well, that when a "fuzzy object" appeared one night in her telescope, she knew that she was seeing something for the first time.

By the end of the nineteenth century and the beginning of the twentieth, technology began to catch up with the curiosity of the astronomers. Telescopes increased in size, thanks to George Hale whose whole life was dedicated to designing and building bigger and bigger telescopes. These advances in telescope construction eventually led to the discovery of objects in the sky that helped Harlow Shapley determine the size of the Milky Way galaxy and helped Edwin Hubble determine distances beyond our galaxy.

The developments in photography made it possible for astronomers to take pictures of the heavens. The women of Harvard College Observatory contributed to the mammoth effort of classifying and cataloging the stars in the sky. Both Williamina

Fleming and Annie Cannon had such phenomenal powers of observation and memory, that they could tell immediately whether a particular star changed from picture to picture. These keen observations led to the discovery of many variable stars and many novae. Students at Harvard College Observatory said that Cecilia Payne-Gaposchkin, the first woman professor of astronomy at Harvard, was like a human astronomical encyclopedia.

The ancient astronomers knew about the sun, the moon, and the patterns of the stars in the sky. They probably would be in awe to learn about galaxies and the intense beauty of these objects that can only be seen with the most powerful of telescopes. Vera Rubin, an observer of galaxies, says, "I sometimes ask myself whether I would be studying galaxies if they were ugly."[1]

For some astronomers, this intense curiosity to find out what is out there has led to a fascination about the possibility of other intelligent beings living somewhere else in the universe. This drive motivated Percival Lowell to spend his whole life searching for intelligent life on Mars. Carl Sagan continues the search for extraterrestrial intelligence in the universe. Sagan also has been responsible for giving science and the discoveries of science back to the people. He says, "Science is a joy. It's not just something for an isolated, remote elite. It's our birthright."[2]

Maria Mitchell

Maria Mitchell

(1818–1889)

Maria Mitchell was born into a Quaker family on Nantucket Island in Massachusetts on August 1, 1818. She was the third child in a family of ten children. William Mitchell, Maria's father, was an amateur astronomer. If the sky was clear, he would climb the stairs to the roof of the family's home with one or more of his children in tow. Maria regularly helped her father with these observations. She would stand on the roof in the blustery night air, calling out seconds from the chronometer as her father recorded daily transits of the stars and planets.[1]

As they watched the stars from the roof, Mitchell and her father had long conversations about far away places and the news brought by the whaling ships returning from New Guinea, the Fiji Islands, and the

South Seas.[2] In the mid-1800s, at the height of the whaling industry, Nantucket was a busy and important harbor. During the day, sailors and merchants would cause the little village center to burst into the colors and sounds of the world's people. At night all was silent. Resting twenty miles off the coast of Massachusetts, the island was calm and peaceful.

As Mitchell grew older she continued to help her father with the nightly observations. A clear night would not go by without at least one sweep of the sky. Even if the house was full of visitors, Mitchell would slip away to the roof, chronometer and record book in hand.[3]

Chronometers and sextants were vital to the whaling families of Nantucket. Chronometers were clocks that kept precisely accurate time and helped sailors locate their longitude. Sextants were instruments used to determine the location of a star in the sky. Sextants helped the sailors locate their latitude. Without these tools navigation in the 1800s would have been impossible.

One day when Mitchell was still a young child, her father had gone to the mainland on business. Captain Bill Chadwick, of the whaling ship *Baltic*, arrived at the family house. Between voyages the captains of the ships would bring their chronometers to Mr. Mitchell to check them for accuracy. Maria Mitchell listened as the captain and her mother discussed the absence of her father. Finally, Maria said timidly, "I can do it, Mother, I'm sure I can, if thee'll only let me try. Thee knows I have often watched father."[4]

Captain Chadwick scowled, but left the chrono-meter. That evening, when the stars came out, the young girl was ready with her sextant and telescope. By the light of a little whale oil lamp, she painstakingly calibrated the chronometer. In the morning when Captain Chadwick arrived to retrieve his chronometer, it had been calibrated exactly as Maria's father would have done it.[5]

Mitchell finished her formal schooling when she was fifteen. At sixteen she became an assistant to her former teacher, Mr. Pierce. The next year, 1835, she decided to start her own school. When the time arrived, Mitchell anxiously awaited her pupils. On that first day of school, among the many children who arrived were three African-American girls who had been denied access to the public school because of their race. She received all students, black and white, large and small, rich and poor.

Often Mitchell, a dedicated teacher, rose before dawn to take her pupils to watch tiny birds hatching, or gathered children after sunset to watch the stars. She was an avid storyteller and took her students on imaginary trips to distant stars and planets.[6]

The year following the opening of her school, Mitchell was invited to become the librarian for the Nantucket Athenaeum, a newly constructed building housing both a lecture hall and a library. She gave up teaching in her little school and took the position of librarian. This was an important turning point in her life.

As librarian Mitchell now had a great deal of time and a valuable resource at her disposal. She was able to spend most of her free time reading. She chose to study mathematics first and read all the books on that subject that the library owned. Mitchell continued to serve as the town's librarian for nearly twenty years, continuing to read and study.

The old men of Nantucket came to the library, more for conversation with Mitchell than to find reading material. On these days she would take out her knitting and spend hours in intense discussion about whaling, abolition, religion, and politics. Mitchell was considered one of the leading intellectual minds of the time.

During this time Mitchell also helped her father map Nantucket. She walked every inch of the island, measuring every nook and cranny, every pond and bog, every rise and fall of the landscape. When the map was finished in 1838, Mitchell was twenty years old and knew the island better than anyone else ever had.[7]

She also knew the heavens and felt intimately connected to the great constellations. She recorded in her diary, December 1854:

> One gets attached . . . to certain midnight apparitions. The Aurora Borealis is always a pleasant companion; a meteor seems to come like a messenger from departed spirits. . . .[8]

Maria Mitchell (right) helped her father, William Mitchell, map Nantucket. By the time the map was finished in 1838, she knew the island better than anyone else ever had.

Mitchell never gave up her nightly observations. Week after week, month after month, she swept the sky in the dark solitude of the Nantucket nights. Mitchell knew where every star belonged, just as she knew each house on Main Street. At 10:30 P.M. on October 1, 1847, she saw a fuzzy object in her telescope that had not been there before. She continued to peer through her telescope. It was a comet. She was sure of it. Down below in the hall she could hear the laughter of the party that she had slipped away from earlier in the evening. She ran down the stairs and whispered in her father's ear, "Father, come quickly, there's a peculiar white body in the field of the telescope."[9]

Mitchell had discovered the first telescopic comet. For her discovery she received a medal from the king of Denmark, who had established the prize. On one side of the medal in Latin it said, "Not in vain do we watch the setting and rising of the stars. October 1, 1847," and around the edge in large capital letters was her name, MITCHELL. Mitchell had made Nantucket as famous in the scientific community as the sea captains had in the whaling industry.

Mitchell's interest in astronomy was not focused solely on comets. She was particularly interested by star colors. She wrote in her diary:

> Those who know Sirius and Betel do not at once perceive that one shines with a brilliant white light and the other burns with a glowing red. . . . We may turn our gaze as we

18

turn a kaleidoscope, and the changes are infinitely more startling, the combinations infinitely more beautiful; no flower garden presents such a variety and such delicacy of shades.[10]

After the discovery of the comet, Mitchell became well-known in scientific circles. For a young woman from Nantucket who rarely ever left the island and only imagined far away places, her life became filled with travel and important people. She was included in many of the astronomical meetings held all over the world.

In 1848 Maria Mitchell was the first woman elected to the American Academy of Arts and the first woman member of the Association for the Advancement of Science. Later she was one of the founders of the American Association for the Advancement of Women.

In 1861 Vassar Female College in Poughkeepsie, New York, was founded. Mitchell, despite her own lack of formal education, was appointed as a professor of astronomy and director of one of the finest observatories in the country. Mitchell's mother had died, her sisters and brothers had grown, so Mitchell moved with her father to Vassar.[11] Maria Mitchell taught at Vassar until her retirement in 1888. She died at home in Lynn, Massachusetts, in 1889.

Percival Lowell

Percival Lowell
(1855–1916)

Percival Lowell was born in Boston, Massachusetts, on March 13, 1855. He was the oldest child of Augustus Lowell and Katharine Lawrence Lowell. The Lowells and the Lawrences were two of the wealthiest and most well-known families in New England.

As a youth, Percival became fascinated with astronomy. Besides his regular school homework, Percival read all that he could find about astronomy. He had his own two-and-a-quarter-inch refracting telescope. Night after night Lowell would take his telescope to the flat roof of his house and look at the planets. He thought even then that he saw the white snow cap on the pole of Mars and the blue-green patches on an orange ground. Even though he pursued other interests, he never lost his love for astronomy. In high school Percival was always near the top of his class and especially excelled in the classics. Lowell's father drove Percival and his siblings to and from school each day. During these drives Mr. Lowell would encourage the children to work at something worthwhile. The only thing that mattered was the work must "be of real significance."[1]

Lowell entered Harvard College in the fall of 1872. While he was a student at Harvard he studied the classics as well as physics and math. He was a very successful student and won a prize in history, as well as in physics.[2] He graduated from Harvard with honors in 1876.

After graduation he worked in his grandfather's cotton mill as a manager. His career as a business-person lasted about seven years, but he was restless. The work of an executive was not for him.[3]

During the next ten years Lowell traveled throughout Europe and Asia. Lowell was particularly interested in the rituals, trances, and miracles of the Shinto religion. In 1894 he published his fourth book about Japan entitled, *Occult Japan or the Way of the Gods.*

Upon returning to the United States in 1894, his interest in astronomy was rekindled when he read about a discovery made by Giovanni Schiaparelli, an Italian astronomer. Schiaparelli had observed fine lines on the planet Mars and had called these lines "canali." These "canali" intrigued Lowell. He wondered if they could have been made by intelligent beings. He was so fascinated by the possibility of life elsewhere in the solar system that he decided to carry on Schiaparelli's work when he learned of Schiaparelli's failing health.[4]

During the same period Lowell had met Professor W. H. Pickering who suggested that the atmosphere of Earth was interfering with observations of the planets. Pickering was concerned with the effect that air currents had on observations.[5]

Lowell decided to explore the possibility of locating an observatory in a part of the country where atmospheric interference would be at a minimum. This idea of a steady rather than a clear atmosphere was new at the time. It was Lowell's idea that it was more important to find a place where the air was steady, with few currents, than to find a location with few clouds.

Lowell was intent on getting an observatory ready for the next time Mars passed close to Earth. He wanted to find a good place where he could make observations " . . . the determination of the physical condition of the planets of our solar system, primarily Mars; the determination of the conditions conducive to the best astronomical observations."[6]

Because the air quality in drier climates offered the possibility of the best site, Arizona was selected as the most promising spot. Eventually the town of Flagstaff, Arizona, was selected. The town was very generous to this adventure and gave Lowell and his partners the necessary land. The observatory was at 7,250 feet above the level of the sea. He installed the largest refracting telescope available at the time. The observatory was completed in six weeks. It was ready when Mars passed close to Earth. Regular observations began on April 23, 1894.

Lowell was overwhelmed with joy. He said in the *Annals of the Lowell Observatory*:

> The results of the year's work surpassed anticipation. Details invisible at the average observatory were presented at times with copper-plate distinctness, and, what is as vital, the markings were seen hour after hour, day after day, month after month.[7]

Lowell felt that the consistency of his observations of Mars was very reliable. From his observations, he formed a general theory concerning the origins of the "canali." He believed that it was possible for some form of life to survive on Mars. He also believed that the inhabitants of Mars had some intelligence that led them to build the long, straight canals.[8]

Lowell studied the sky every night for a year. He observed most of the night and wrote reports and articles for publication during the day. He recorded his observations and drawings of Mars in great detail. He had noticed that in the winter of the Martian southern hemisphere, there was a region around that pole that turned white. He suggested that it became covered by a mantle of what appeared to be snow or ice. In the Martian summer the supposed snow disappeared altogether. He also described very thin straight lines that appeared to cross the lighter-reddish regions. Lowell was convinced that these lines could not be natural. Someone or something was building these canals. He was more convinced than ever that the canals were built by intelligent creatures.[9]

In November 1895, after a year of almost nightly observations, he wrote a book entitled *Mars*. In this book he explained his theory about the possible existence of intelligent life on Mars. He came to this conclusion in trying to explain the intersections of the lines. He thought these intersections to be like "oases." He said:

> We find . . . the broad physical conditions of the planet are not antagonistic to some form of life . . . there is an apparent dearth of water upon the planet's surface . . . there turns out to be a network of markings covering the disk precisely counterparting what a system of irrigation would look like . . . there is a set of spots placed where we should expect to find the lands thus artificially fertilized . . . All this, of course, may be a set of coincidences, signifying nothing; but the probability points the other way.[10]

Lowell believed that the "seeing" in Arizona was so good that he decided to build a permanent observatory there. He installed a twenty-four-inch refracting telescope. The site of the observatory became known as Mars Hill. Lowell also built a small home near the observatory.

Lowell is most remembered for the controversy he created about intelligent life on Mars. In 1907 at the height of the Mars furor, the *Wall Street Journal*

Percival Lowell installed a twenty-four-inch refracting telescope in his observatory. The site of the observatory was known as "Mars Hill."

said that the "most extraordinary event of the last twelve months was the proof afforded by astronomical observations that conscious, intelligent human life exists upon the planet Mars."[11] Lowell never said "human life," but he did say, "intelligent life."

Most of Lowell's theories have been disproved by recent developments in astronomy. However, Lowell made many other contributions to the field of astronomy. He established a major observatory, and he was an early advocate for another planet outside the orbit of Neptune. Others had speculated about a ninth planet, but Lowell set about finding it. He established a careful observation program in search of Planet X. Photographic surveys of the sky in the region where Planet X was predicted to be were systematically undertaken. For a time after Lowell's death in 1916, the search for Planet X was abandoned but was later renewed at the Lowell Observatory. On March 13, 1930, on what would have been Lowell's seventy-fifth birthday, an announcement was made that Clyde Tombaugh had found Planet X. The planet was named Pluto and the symbol PL was chosen for this new planet in honor of Percival Lowell.[12]

Lowell was a dedicated observer of the planets. Although his theories about intelligent life on Mars have been proven false by recent research, his contribution in the history of astronomy cannot be ignored.

Lowell died of a stroke in his observatory in 1916.

Williamina Fleming

Williamina Fleming

(1857–1911)

Williamina Stevens was born in Dundee, Scotland, in 1857. Her father, Robert, was a woodcarver and photographer. He died in 1864 leaving the family in financial difficulties. When Williamina was fourteen, she became a teacher to help support her family and taught for five years. At nineteen she and her new husband, James Orr Fleming, traveled to the United States where they made their new home. Unfortunately, the marriage only lasted two years. At the time of her divorce Williamina was about to give birth to her only child. Finding herself nearly destitute, she became a maid to Edward C. Pickering, who was the director of the Harvard College Observatory.[1] This contact with Pickering was the turning point in her life that led her to a career in astronomy.

Pickering realized that Fleming had more potential than was required for a maid and invited her to join the staff at Harvard as a "computer" in 1881. Pickering was in the process of cataloging the stars and hired many women for this painstaking work. Williamina Fleming was one of the women. Although Fleming had no formal training in astronomy, she possessed the qualities that were required to be a human "computer." She was diligent; she had exceptional eyesight; and she had a remarkable memory.[2]

Observational astronomy was on the edge of great change. Part of this change came about because new tools like cameras and spectrographs became available to astronomers. A spectrograph is a device that uses a prism to separate white light into different colors. Astronomers began to look at the spectra produced when the light from stars passed through the prism. They noticed patterns of dark lines in the spectra. They also knew that the gasses of elements like hydrogen and oxygen produced special patterns of dark lines. Because each element had its own unique set of lines, astronomers were able to tell what elements were in each star.

The spectra of many of the stars in the sky were recorded on photographic plates like pictures. On each plate there were hundreds of tiny spectra all different from one another. Fleming was in charge of these plates. Her task was to classify each star according to its unique spectra or pattern of dark lines. In addition, it was her job to take care of the plates. Each photographic plate was very valuable and very fragile.[3]

Fleming created a classification system using fifteen different color patterns and named them using most of the letters from A to Q. The system of classification developed by Fleming was a major contribution to astronomy which was further refined by Annie Jump Cannon in later years.[4]

Fleming began her career at Harvard as one of the "computers." Gradually she took on more responsibilities, eventually becoming the supervisor of the other women "computers." She was a very efficient administrator. Not only was she responsible for the classification of the stars and the supervision of the workers, but she was also responsible for the compilation of the *Draper Catalog of Stellar Spectra*. It was a momentous undertaking. Fleming edited the catalog. It was published in 1890.

Fleming discovered a new way to identify long-period variable stars. Variable stars are stars that change in brightness. Long-period variables are the largest group of these stars. They are giant stars with long and often irregular periods.

Fleming identified 222 variable stars and presented her work to astronomers in 1907. Many astronomers were skeptical of the new photographic methods. They suggested that the variation in the

Williamina Fleming (standing) became the supervisor of the women "computers" at Harvard University.

brightness of stars was due to faulty technique or equipment. Fleming stood firm on her observations, however, claiming that the changes on the photographs were caused by the stars and not by the telescopes.

A British astronomer, H. H. Turner, remarked about Fleming, "Many astronomers are deservedly proud to have discovered one variable . . . the discovery of 222 [variables] . . . is an achievement bordering on the marvelous."[5]

The Harvard Observatory had a station in Peru, set up to observe the parts of the sky not seen from the northern hemisphere. One October, while Fleming was examining a plate made at the Peru station, she thought she saw a star in one of the constellations that was not there before. A plate of the region taken three weeks earlier showed no trace of the star. She had discovered a nova. A nova is a star that suddenly becomes hundreds to thousands of times brighter than it was before. In the next few years she discovered other novae. In all, Fleming discovered ten novae, accounting for more than one-third of the novae that were known at the time.[6]

The search for variable stars created a competitive spirit among the Harvard staff that was not always friendly. The researchers in Peru who were taking the photographs usually just shipped the plates to Harvard. There Fleming and the other women would do the analysis and cataloging. It became routine for Fleming to discover variable stars. Some of the observers in Peru wanted the credit for the discoveries. They started analyzing and marking the plates in Peru before they were shipped back to Massachusetts. Fleming was not pleased with this arrangement because she ultimately had to do all the work and analysis on the objects over again.[7] She still had to measure the positions, the variations in brightness, identify the spectrum, and classify the object. If the astronomers in Peru had identified a "suspected" peculiar object, they wanted the credit for the original discovery.

In addition to her other duties, Fleming served as editor for all the publications issued by Harvard College Observatory. In 1898 she was appointed curator of astronomical photographs. She examined and cataloged nearly two hundred thousand photographic plates from 1882 to 1910. She kept to a schedule of long hours, denying herself vacations, and for thirty years hardly missed a day of work.[8]

During her life Williamina Fleming received many honors. In 1906 Fleming became the first American woman to be elected to the Royal Astronomical Society. She was also made an honorary fellow in astronomy at Wellesley College. The Astronomical Society of Mexico presented her with the Guadeloupe Almendaro medal for her discovery of new stars. She was a member of the Astronomical and Astrophysical Society of America and the Société

Astronomique de France. Annie Jump Cannon said of her:

> Mrs. Fleming was possessed of an extremely magnetic personality and an attractive countenance. . . . Although most of her life was spent in the routine of science, yet her human interests were numerous. Fond of people and excitement, there was no more enthusiastic spectator in the stadium for the football games. . . . Industrious by nature, she was seldom idle, and long years of observatory work never unfitted her for the domestic side of life. . . . She was never too tired to welcome her friends at her home or at the observatory, with that quality of human sympathy. . . . Her bright face, her attractive manner, and her cheery greeting with its charming Scotch accent, will long be remembered.[9]

Fleming was particularly interested in the stars that had peculiar spectra, the stars that did not fall easily into the classification system. She discovered 94 of the 107 known Wolf-Rayet stars. Wolf-Rayet stars are a rare group of small, hot stars that are surrounded by a cloud of gaseous material that has been ejected by the star. Before her death, she was working on a portion of the *Annals of the Harvard College Observatory* called "Peculiar Spectra."[10] When she died she left enough unfinished material to fill several volumes of the *Annals.*[11]

After working for Pickering for thirty years, Fleming died in 1911 at the age of fifty-four, leaving her only son, Edward.

Annie Jump Cannon

Annie Jump Cannon
(1863-1941)

Annie Jump Cannon was born in Dover, Delaware, on December 11, 1863, to a prominent family. Her father, Wilson Lee Cannon, a shipbuilder by trade, was also Lieutenant Governor of Delaware. During his term prior to the Civil War, he cast the tie-breaking vote that kept Delaware in the Union.

Annie's interest in astronomy came from her mother. When Annie was a child her mother would tell her wonderful stories about the constellations. A constellation is a group of stars that appear to represent a picture in the sky. Ancient peoples named these sky pictures. In the evening, young Cannon climbed to the roof of her house through a trapdoor in the attic.[1] Here she studied the stars with the help of her mother's old astronomy book. These nightly observations provided the foundation for what was later to become one of Cannon's greatest skills, keen and accurate observation.

Along with her brothers and sisters, Cannon attended Dover Academy. Her teacher convinced Mr. Cannon that Annie should go to college because she was an exceptional student. Mr. Cannon selected Wellesley College in Massachusetts for his daughter.[2] She was only sixteen when she left home. Her college years were filled with frequent colds and flu, probably from the cold New England weather. This eventually led to the deafness that began when she was a young women.

During her college years she never took an astronomy course. However, she did study physics with Professor Sarah F. Whiting and graduated with a degree in science. Whiting's enthusiasm for spectroscopy inspired Cannon.[3]

After college Annie moved back home to Delaware to live with her family. There she formed many reading groups around the Dover area. For twelve years she enjoyed the simple social life of home and community. When her mother died in 1894 Cannon said, referring to the stars, "In troubled days it is good to have something outside our planet, something fine and distant for comfort."[4] Without the friendship of her mother, Cannon became restless. In her journal she recorded, "I am sometimes very dissatisfied with life here. I do want to accomplish something so badly. There are so many things that I could do if only I had the money."[5]

Cannon finally returned to Wellesley College as an assistant in the physics department. In 1895 she formally began her study of astronomy as a special student at Radcliffe College in Cambridge, Massachusetts. At Radcliffe she met Dr. Edward Pickering, the director of the Harvard University Observatory. Pickering was directing a project to classify the stars in the sky. In 1896 Cannon joined Pickering on this project and began her career as a scientist and astronomer. She was thirty-four years old.

The spectra of stars brighter than ninth magnitude were being photographed by the astronomers at the Harvard College Observatory. Thousands of stars were to be classified according to their spectra. Many systems had been tried, but a better system of classification was needed. Cannon's keen visual memory qualified her to sort out these line patterns and to place each star in its proper category. Williamina Fleming had created a classification system based on fifteen categories named alphabetically from A to Q. Some of the categories had few or no stars in them. Cannon arranged and rearranged these categories. Eventually she discovered a way to sort and classify the stars by their physical properties.

She rearranged the categories from the hottest stars to the coolest stars rather than alphabetically. The new sequence using Fleming's original letter designations became OBAFGKM. This sequence for categorizing stars was adopted by the International Astronomical Union. The new order laid the groundwork for modern stellar spectroscopy.[6]

Between 1911 and 1915 Cannon classified 5,000 stars per month. For sparsely populated regions of the sky, Cannon could classify more than three stars a minute. Cannon had great skill at seeing unusual things. Her particularly sharp eyesight was needed to interpret what was on each photographic plate.

Between 1918 and 1924 nine volumes of the Henry Draper Catalog were published. The catalog listed the spectral classification of 225,000 stars, each star's position in the sky, and each star's visual and photographic brightness. This catalog is very valuable to astronomers because of its consistency. It is consistent because it is the result of the work of one person.[7] These catalogs are referred to as "the bible of modern astronomy."[8]

Dr. Harlow Shapley, director of the Harvard College Observatory, said:

> Miss Cannon had a phenomenal memory. When I went to her office the first day . . . I said . . . 'I'd like to see the spectrum of SW Andromedae.' (That was a faint variable-star spectrum that I had a hunch about.) She called to her assistant 'Will you get Plate I 37311?' She just sang out that five-figure number. The girl went to the stacks and got the plate and SW Andromedae was on it![9]

This story clearly shows that she had a wonderful memory for details.

Between 1911 and 1915, Annie Jump Cannon classified 5,000 stars per month. She could sometimes classify more than three stars per minute.

During her career as an astronomer, Annie Jump Cannon classified nearly four hundred thousand stars. She is responsible for the discovery of three hundred variable stars. A variable star is a star that varies in brightness. She also discovered five novae. A nova is a star that suddenly blazes up with a great increase in brightness.

In 1907 she compiled a catalog of 1,380 variables, and in 1926 helped publish a list of 1,760 long-period variables. She maintained an ever-expanding card index of the literature of variable stars. This card index was of great value to her colleagues at Harvard as well as many other astronomers.

In 1911 Cannon was appointed curator of astronomical photographs at the observatory. While Cannon was at the observatory, she undertook the project of sorting all stars down to the ninth magnitude. That is about a quarter of a million objects in all. The magnitude of a star is a measure of the star's brightness. The brightest stars in the sky are said to be "first" magnitude stars. Sixth magnitude stars are less bright and barely visible to the naked eye.

In addition to her career as an astronomer, Cannon traveled extensively and played music. She had an engaging personality and had many friends. Because many people perceived her to be good company, her friends included all kinds of people, old and young, astronomers and non-astronomers alike.[10]

She was the recipient of the first honorary degree in science ever awarded to a woman by England's Oxford University. The degree was to honor her for her unique contribution to the new science of astrophysics. At the time she was one of only six people who had been made honorary members of the Royal Astronomical Society of England since that society's origin in 1820. She also received the first gold medal awarded a woman by America's National Academy of Sciences. In addition to the honorary degree from Oxford University she received five other honorary degrees.

When Cannon was seventy-five years old, the Harvard Board of Overseers finally honored her by appointing her their William Cranch Bond Astronomer. As early as 1911, the Visiting Committee to the Observatory wrote of Cannon, "It is an anomaly that, though she is recognized the world over as the greatest living expert in this line of work, and her services to the Observatory are so important, yet she holds no official position in the university."[11]

Cannon established the Annie Jump Cannon Prize for women astronomers.

Annie Jump Cannon died in 1941.

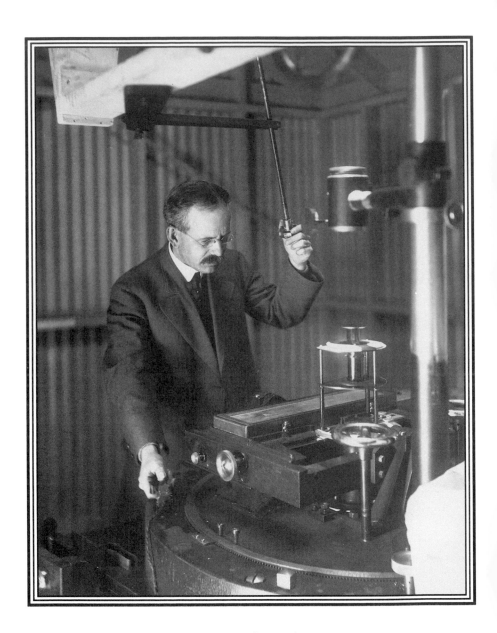

George Ellery Hale

George Ellery Hale

(1868–1938)

George Ellery Hale was born in 1868 in Chicago, Illinois. His father, William Hale, a wealthy manufacturer, encouraged in George an intense energy, and an interest in engineering. His mother helped develop his imagination by reading with him.[1]

As a boy George did not like school. He had "an aversion to the confinements and the fixed duties of school life."[2] Instead of going to school, he wanted personal adventure. He preferred to work at things he liked. Tools and machinery fascinated him when he was young, and he always had a small shop with many tools wherever he lived. He also had a little laboratory where he performed simple chemical experiments. Being curious about planets, he tried to make his own telescope. When his father saw his interest in telescopes, he bought his son a four-inch Clark telescope.

Hale said:

> . . . my enthusiasm reached the highest pitch when I learned something about the spectroscope. My greatest ambition was to photograph a spectrum [of the sun] . . . Solar spectroscopic work appealed to me above all things and I read everything I could find on the subject.[3]

A spectroscope can be attached to a telescope. The light from the star passes through a prism in the spectroscope. When white light passes through a prism, the light is seen as a rainbow. This rainbow is called a spectrum. The narrow, dark-line patterns within the rainbow of each star identify the elements present in the star.

Hale made his first small, one-prism spectroscope in 1884 when he was sixteen. His father's policy was to encourage George to construct his own instrument first and then give him a good instrument if the early experiments were successful.

In 1886 George entered the Massachusetts Institute of Technology in Cambridge, Massachusetts. He majored in physics.[4] In his spare time he would go to the Boston Public Library. There he read everything he could find on astronomy and spectroscopy. He also volunteered as an assistant at the Harvard Observatory.[5]

In 1888 William Hale built his son his own spectroscopic laboratory behind the Hale home in

Chicago, known as the Kenwood Observatory. George Hale continued to struggle with the difficult problem of photographing the sun. The sun was too bright to photograph easily. The next summer when he was twenty-one, the solution came while he was riding on a Chicago trolley car. He said that it just came to him "out of the blue."

He created the spectroheliograph. A spectroheliograph is an instrument that takes pictures of the sun showing the sun's faculae and prominences. Faculae are bright regions of the sun, usually seen near the apparent edge of the sun as seen in the sky. A prominence looks like a flame above the edge of the sun. In 1889 he tried out his spectroheliograph at the Harvard Observatory.[6]

Hale graduated from the Massachusetts Institute of Technology on June 1, 1890. He married Evelina Conklin two days later. On their honeymoon they traveled to the West Coast and the Lick Observatory of the University of California at San Jose.

At the Lick Observatory, Edward Holden, the director, allowed Hale to attach his spectroheliograph to the thirty-six-inch telescope, the largest telescope in the world at the time. Hale was very impressed with what "modern engineering, in the hands of a master, can do for astronomy."[7] This big telescope allowed him to take better pictures of the sun.

Hale decided to return to Chicago to develop his plan for photographing the sun's prominences with a new twelve-inch refracting telescope. Finally, in

1892, Hale photographed the prominences around the sun's apparent edge for the first time.

In 1892 he was appointed associate professor of astrophysics at the newly opened University of Chicago. While he was there, he learned of the availability of two forty-inch telescope lenses. He knew that these lenses could be used to build a large telescope. He wanted a telescope "that would carry powerful spectroscopes and spectroheliographs and give large pictures of the sun suitable for the study of sun spots, faculae and prominences."[8]

It was difficult to get enough money to build the telescope because the new university needed money for other things. Hale had to find someone outside of the university to give money for the telescope. He went to a businessperson, Charles Yerkes, for money and Yerkes agreed to buy the forty-inch lens. However, because the university was still trying to finance its other building projects, it would not fund the construction of a building to house the new telescope. Eventually Yerkes agreed to build the complete observatory building when Hale agreed to raise the money needed for operating expenses. Construction began in 1895.

On October 21, 1897, the Yerkes Observatory was dedicated at Williams Bay, Wisconsin. The new observatory was revolutionary. Hale said, "In reality it is a large physical laboratory as well as an astronomical establishment" where "all kinds of spectroscopic, bolometric, photographic and other optical work could be done in the laboratories."[9]

A special meeting of astronomers was held at the Yerkes Observatory dedication in 1897. Two years later the first meeting of the new American Astronomical Society was held at Yerkes Observatory.

While Hale was directing the building and operation of the Yerkes Observatory, he gathered a small but devoted staff. He continued to observe sunspot spectra, and designed a spectroheliograph that was attached to the forty-inch telescope.

In 1896 Hale persuaded his father to provide the curved mirror for a sixty-inch reflecting telescope so he could photograph the spectral patterns of stars. William Hale had offered this mirror to the University of Chicago on the condition that funds be found to build the rest of the telescope. The attempts to find enough money were unsuccessful, and the mirror remained in the Yerkes Observatory basement.

In 1904, after overcoming many difficulties and investing $30,000 of his own money, Hale moved to Pasadena, California, where he founded the Mount Wilson Solar Observatory on December 20, 1904.

In 1905 Hale photographed a sunspot spectrum. Hale's observations proved that sunspots were cooler areas on the sun. Unfortunately, the warm days and cool nights in California were causing difficulties with the telescopes. Finally, in 1908 Hale solved the problem of the temperature changes. He designed a sixty-foot tower for the telescope and put the spectrograph in a pit underground.

George Ellery Hale (right) shows his sixty-inch telescope on Mount Wilson to businessperson Andrew Carnegie.

Hale was still trying to answer the question: Is the sun itself a magnet? His desire to learn more about the sun drove him to build a bigger telescope.

When Hale went to California, he had taken the sixty-inch reflector given by his father. In 1908, twelve years after his father had given him the mirror, the sixty-inch reflecting telescope, the largest in the world, was set up on Mount Wilson.

The sixty-inch telescope only made Hale want a larger telescope. He persuaded businessperson John Hooker to donate funds for a one-hundred-inch mirror. This mirror was installed in a telescope in 1917. This telescope was responsible for contributions later made by Edwin Hubble.[10]

Hale never was satisfied. He wanted an even larger telescope and this desire drove him to plan a two-hundred-inch reflecting telescope. The Rockefeller Foundation provided the funds and Mount Palomar was picked as the site for the new observatory. Hale did not live to see the culmination of his dream. He died in 1938, ten years before the two-hundred-inch Palomar telescope was completed.

Hale has been called the "master builder" in recognition of his role in the building of large telescopes. He should also be remembered as a pioneer in understanding the physics of the sun. In 1970 the Mount Wilson and Palomar Observatories were renamed the Hale Observatories in his honor.

Harlow Shapley

Harlow Shapley
(1885–1972)

Harlow Shapley was born on a farm near Carthage, Missouri, in 1885. His father was a hay producer and dealer. Harlow and his twin brother attended a one-room schoolhouse near their farm for a few years. Except for this one-room school, Shapley had no regular schooling until he was in his teens. For a few months when he was fifteen, he attended a business school. This led to a brief career as a crime reporter for the Chanute, Kansas, *Daily Sun* newspaper when he was sixteen.

It was in Chanute that he first saw a public library. Because the family was poor, books had never been part of Shapley's early years. At the Chanute Library Shapley started to read history and poetry. Shapley decided "to get educated" and go to high school. He and his younger brother, John, tried to enroll in the Carthage, Missouri, high school, but were turned down because they were not qualified.

This rejection did not stop Shapley. He was determined to further his education. He soon found a Presbyterian-run school, the Carthage Collegiate Institute, that accepted him as a student. He was the top student in a class of three students. Shapley taught himself Latin, geometry, and Greek. Eventually he entered the University of Missouri in Columbia. He says, "From then on I was never stopped. . . ."[1]

Shapley planned to study journalism, but as fate would have it, the journalism program at the university was not ready for students. Undaunted by this disappointing turn of events, Shapley looked in the college catalog for help. The first course listed was archaeology. He could not pronounce the word and had only a vague notion of what it meant. The next course listed in the catalog was astronomy. At least he knew what astronomy was, so he took the course. Shapley earned his bachelor's and master's degrees in astronomy in four years at the University of Missouri. During his college career, even though Shapley was the only astronomy major, his interest was primarily in the classics.

At the university Shapley met Frederick Seares, a professor of astronomy. Seares recognized the spark in Shapley and recommended him for a fellowship at Princeton University in New Jersey.

During his studies at Princeton, Henry Norris Russell, a professor of astronomy, influenced Shapley. Part of Shapely's work at Princeton included making nearly ten thousand observations of eclipsing binary stars. Binary stars are two stars that are going around an imaginary point between them. Almost half of the stars we see in the sky are binary stars. An eclipsing binary star system is a pair of stars arranged so that it looks as if one star passes in front of the other star. When one star blocks the light from the other star, it looks to people on Earth as if the star is suddenly becoming dimmer.

Cepheids are another kind of star that vary in brightness. Many astronomers believed that Cepheids were a special type of binary star system. Shapley showed that Cepheids could not be binary stars. He claimed that Cepheids are actually single supergiant stars that "are throbbing or vibrating masses of gas."[2] To observers on Earth this pulsating causes the star to change brightness.

Seares continued to help Shapley throughout his career. In 1913 Seares eventually persuaded George Hale, director of the Mount Wilson Observatory in California, to hire Shapley. After completing his studies at Princeton, Shapley joined Frederick Seares and George Hale at the Mount Wilson Observatory. Shapley helped Seares observe the colors and brightness of stars. The magnitude of a star is a measure of the brightness of the star. While Shapley was working at Mount Wilson, he was able to use the sixty-inch reflecting telescope a few nights a month. This was the biggest telescope in the world at the time.

When he was not working with Seares on star magnitudes, he devoted much of his own research to Cepheid variable stars and globular clusters. A globular cluster looks like a fuzzy sphere of light. Globular clusters are hundreds of thousands of stars grouped together. These groups of stars are generally found near the middle of galaxies.

Another astronomer at Harvard, Henrietta Leavitt, noticed that for Cepheid stars the longer it took for the star to change from dim to bright to dim, the brighter the star was.[3] This discovery made it possible to determine the distance to Cepheid stars. By taking Leavitt's discovery into account, Shapley was able to measure the distance to the Cepheid stars in the globular clusters near the middle of our galaxy. The Milky Way galaxy is the galaxy where we live. By using Cepheid stars, he calculated that a typical globular cluster could be nearly fifty thousand light-years away. A light-year is the distance light travels in one year. Astronomers use light-years to measure very large distances. Shapley showed that the center of the Milky Way was tens of thousands of light-years away. He also showed that the sun and our solar system are not at the center of the galaxy, but about fifty thousand light-years from the center.

Some of the other astronomers at the time thought that these distances were much too large. They tried very hard to disprove Shapley's theory. In

Harlow Shapley was first appointed astronomer, then director of the Harvard College Observatory.

1921 Shapley and Curtis, of Lick Observatory, had a "great debate" at the annual spring meeting of the National Academy of Sciences. Shapely's position was that the Milky Way galaxy was very large, while Curtis held the old view that the Milky Way was much smaller. On this point Shapley was right. Shapley changed the way astronomers thought about our galaxy.

After seven years at Mount Wilson, Shapley was first appointed astronomer and then director of the Harvard College Observatory in Cambridge, Massachusetts. During Shapley's tenure at the Harvard College Observatory, many changes took place. By the late 1920s students from around the world enrolled in Harvard's astronomy programs. The first person to receive a Ph.D. in astronomy was Cecilia Payne. Shapley also updated the equipment at the observatory. In 1932 a sixty-one-inch telescope was dedicated.

Shapley was one of the people primarily responsible for the establishment of the National Science Foundation. The purpose of the foundation was to get government money to pay for scientific research.

In 1945 Shapley and others created what eventually became UNESCO (United Nations Educational, Scientific, and Cultural Organization). He attended the meeting in London as the official American scientist and contributed to the writing of the charter for this organization.

Shapley wrote several books. He said his favorite was *Of Stars and Men* that he wrote in 1958. He received honorary degrees from seventeen institutions and was a member of many associations and societies around the world.[4]

Shapley died in 1972.

Edwin Hubble

7

Edwin Hubble
(1889–1953)

Edwin Hubble was born on November 20, 1889, in Marshfield, Missouri. His father, John Hubble, was an insurance agent. Edwin Hubble was the third of seven children in the Hubble family. During his elementary school years, the family moved several times as John Hubble's work moved.

Hubble was a good student and a fine athlete. He was a member of his high school's track team and won the high jump at Northwestern Interscholastic meet with a leap of six feet one-quarter inches. When Hubble was sixteen, he graduated from Wheaton High School in Wheaton, Illinois.[1]

He entered the University of Chicago on a scholarship. Hubble's college career showed good academic work. He continued his interest in sports, winning letters in track and basketball. Hubble graduated from the University of Chicago in 1910 with a Bachelor of Science degree at the age of twenty.

Hubble continued his studies at Queens College in Oxford, England, as a Rhodes Scholar. At Queens he studied law, a profession that had been chosen for him by his father and grandfather. He returned to the United States intending to become a lawyer. He even passed the Kentucky bar exam. However, there is no evidence that he ever practiced law. Instead he taught Spanish and physics in the high school at New Albany, Indiana.

Even though he was a very popular teacher and coach, he went back to graduate school in Chicago to study astronomy. As a student he began work at Yerkes Observatory located in the village of Williams Bay in southern Wisconsin.

While at Yerkes Observatory, Hubble attended a meeting of the American Astronomical Society where an astronomer, V. M. Slipher, presented his latest observations of M31. M31 is a fuzzy spot in the sky known as the Andromeda nebula. Many astronomers considered that nebulae were large amounts of dust and gas. Slipher was one of the first people to obtain a clearly exposed spectrogram of a spiral nebula.

When an element is heated it is identified by a pattern in the colors of the rainbow shown by the spectrograph. Each element has its own unique set of colors. This set of colors is called a spectrogram.

When an object is moving away from Earth, the lines on its spectrum are shifted toward the red end of the rainbow. When an object is moving toward Earth, the lines are shifted toward the blue end. These shifts are called Doppler shifts. The spectrogram of M31 showed that the galaxy was approaching the sun. Slipher obtained spectra of many more galaxies. He found that most of them are moving away from the sun.

Excited by Slipher's presentation, Hubble began his own study of nebular photography.[2] This interest led to Hubble's research for his Ph.D. thesis, *Photographic Investigations of Faint Nebulae.* In this work he described and classified numerous small, faint "nebulae." He found that most of the nebulae were not in the Milky Way galaxy. He showed that many of them were far away galaxies similar to our own galaxy, while some were huge clouds of gas within our galaxy. This work marked the beginnings of his later research about galaxies and the whole universe.

In 1916 Hubble met George Hale, the director of Mount Wilson Observatory. Hale had heard about the bright young student who was doing an observational thesis on nebulae with the twenty-four-inch reflecting telescope and offered Hubble a job. However, the move to Mount Wilson had to wait. America was entering World War I and Hubble joined the army. He volunteered for the infantry and became a captain. At his commanding officer's request, he taught his fellow trainees how to do night marching by watching the stars. He was promoted from captain to major in 1918.

When the war ended, Hubble wrote to George Hale and asked if the invitation to work at Mount Wilson was still open. Hale said:

> Please come as soon as possible as we expect to get the one-hundred-inch telescope working very soon, and there should be abundant opportunity for work by the time you arrive.[3]

The timing was perfect. Even though the one-hundred-inch telescope had been built in 1917, use of it was postponed by the war. General use of this telescope by the staff began a few days after Hubble's arrival in 1919. From his experience at Yerkes, he knew how to use reflecting telescopes. He knew about nebulae, and he knew about the problems that needed solving. He went right to work trying to determine the distance to these nebulae.

Humason, a staff member at Mount Wilson, says about Hubble in those first days:

> I received a vivid impression of the man that night that has remained with me over the years. He was photographing at the Newtonian focus of the 60-inch, standing while he did his guiding. His tall, vigorous figure, pipe in mouth, was clearly outlined against the sky. A brisk wind whipped his military trench coat around his body and occasionally blew sparks from his pipe into the darkness of the dome. "Seeing" that night was rated as extremely poor on our

Mount Wilson scale, but when Hubble came back from developing his plate he was jubilant. "If this is a sample of poor seeing conditions," he said, "I shall always be able to get usable photographs with the Mount Wilson instruments." The confidence and enthusiasm which he showed on that night were typical of the way he approached all his problems. He was sure of himself—of what he wanted to do, and of how to do it.[4]

Using photographs of nebulae, Hubble found Cepheid variable stars. Cepheid variables are yellow supergiant pulsating stars that are very important in establishing distances to groups of stars beyond our galaxy. He analyzed the light of Cepheid stars in three nebulae.[5] By using these Cepheid stars with Shapley's technique, Hubble was able to determine the distance to these galaxies. This discovery was very important. It was the missing piece in a long-continuing puzzle about the size of the universe.

Slipher had already shown that most galaxies are moving away from ours. However, Hubble used the spectrograph to show a relationship between the distance and velocity of galaxies. His results showed that the farther away a galaxy is from us, the faster it is moving away. This shocking evidence that the universe is expanding changed the centuries-old opinion that the universe was static.

Hubble announced a classification scheme for galaxies in the 1920s. By the 1930s he had become

Edwin Hubble worked with the 100-inch telescope at Mount Wilson. He announced a classification scheme for galaxies in the 1920s.

famous. The Hubble atlas of galaxies was published in the early 1960s. Characteristic of Hubble's science is an early focus upon crucial issues and an unrelenting pursuit of them. Hubble's wife, Grace, says:

> I think it was in the 1930s when about every two weeks some of the men from Mount Wilson and Cal Tech came to the house in the evening. They brought a blackboard and put it up on the living room wall. . . . Sitting around the fire, smoking pipes, they talked over various approaches to problems, questioned, compared and contrasted their points of view. Someone would write equations on the blackboard and talk for a bit, and a discussion would follow.[6]

Hubble soon became the outstanding observational cosmologist in the country. He gave the first evidence for the expansion of the universe. Hubble changed our view of the universe more than any astronomer since Galileo. Hubble's drive, scientific ability, and communication skills enabled him to seize the problem of the whole universe and make it peculiarly his own.

Hubble died in 1953. When NASA launched a satellite with a special space telescope attached, they named it the Hubble Space Telescope in honor of Edwin Hubble.

Cecilia Payne-Gaposchkin

Cecilia
Payne-Gaposchkin

(1900–1979)

Cecilia Payne was born in England in 1900. Her father, Edward Payne, was a lawyer, a historian, and a gifted musician. When he was fifty-five he married Emma Pertz, an accomplished artist. Edward Payne died five years later leaving his wife with three small children, Cecilia, Humfry, and Lenora. Mrs. Payne insisted that all three of her children attend college. She accomplished this with very little money or help from others.[1]

As a young child Cecilia Payne attended a school where she learned about the Bible, the catechism, and the history of the church. The atmosphere was stifling to her. She hated going to chapel every day and finally succeeded in getting excused from daily chapel by pretending to faint.[2]

Payne loved math and science, but very little science was taught in her school. She decided to concentrate on subjects that would help her reach her goal of being a scientist. It was uphill work in that school.[3]

She chose to take her education into her own hands. In her spare time, she translated a German-French botany book into English. She also studied the writings of Isaac Newton and Swedenborg's *Chemistry, Physics, Philosophy.* She says that Swedenborg's work gave her "a mystical view" of science that she never lost.[4]

Her school held the nineteenth-century view that science and religion were in conflict. She wanted desperately to be a scientist. She wrote:

> At the time when I left this school, openly resolved to be a scientist, the Principal . . . told me that I was "prostituting my gifts". . . . To her the chapel was more important than the laboratory.

> But by this time I had, in a sense, converted the laboratory into a chapel. On the top floor of the school . . . was a room set aside for the little science teaching conceded to the upper classes. The chemicals were ranged in bottles round the walls. I used to steal up there by myself . . . and sit conducting a little worship service of my own, adoring the chemical elements. . . . [5]

She did find one teacher that understood her desire to be a scientist, Dorothy Dalglish. Dalglish taught Payne botany and chemistry and loaned her books on physics. Dalglish also helped Payne develop an interest in botany. Instead of just making a plant collection, Dalglish instructed Payne to make careful drawings of what she saw. She made precise drawings of many different plants.[6]

Payne developed incredible powers of observation as well as skill in accurate drawing. Through the development of this set of botanical drawings, Payne also acquired a thorough knowledge of botany.

When Miss Dalglish left the school, Payne continued her uphill struggle for a scientific education in a school that wanted her to be trained in the classics.[7] Her interest in science did not keep her from doing excellent work in other fields of study. Payne won a school prize given at the end of the year. When she was asked what book she wanted for a prize, she chose a science book about fungi.[8]

Against everyone's advice, she took the botany college entrance exam. She passed the exam with top honors. She was determined to be a botanist, but she had little support. She wrote:

> The next few years were a confused and unhappy time. I insisted that I must learn advanced mathematics and German for (both would be necessary to a scientist), and no other girl in the school had any such needs or requirements. Most of the pupils were destined for the social world, and several became successful actresses. Few went on to College.[9]

She found someone to tutor her in German. She also studied calculus and geometry by herself. Unfortunately the school assigned her to a ". . . stern, ascetic teacher of mathematics . . ." who ". . . drove me into a nervous frenzy, and produced a block about the subject that I have never completely overcome. . . ." [10]

Her education was not going well and finally the school asked her to leave. She thought that her world had ended. She was almost seventeen, and she wanted to go to college. She thought when she was told to leave that the fates had destroyed her life, but the fates had opened a new path for her.

She soon entered St. Paul's Girls School. This school had laboratories for biology, physics, and chemistry and teachers who were specialists in their sciences. Girls were encouraged to study science. In her autobiography Payne says that:

> As I look back I see that life began for me when I entered the doors from Brook Green, Hammersmith. It was a time of dynamic happiness. I remember saying to myself: I shall never be lonely again; now I can think about science. [11]

At this school Payne thrived. She studied both science and music. Science was still her primary love. For the first time she really studied physics. [12]

Physics soon replaced botany as her favorite science:

> All motion, I had learned, was relative. Suddenly, as I was walking down a London street I asked myself: 'relative to what?' The solid ground failed beneath my feet. With

the familiar leaping of my heart I had my
first sense of the Cosmos.[13]

To enter college at Cambridge, England, she had to
pass examinations in math, Latin, and Greek. One of
the test questions required translating a passage from
the Bible into English. Her early religious training
finally became useful. She knew the passage. Instead of
writing a translation, she just wrote it from memory.

After a lecture on Einstein's theories during her first
year at Cambridge, she decided to become an astronomer. She had very little financial support so she
searched for sources of money. She found a prize
offered for the best essay on one of the Greek passages
in the gospels. She used the money she won from this
prize for traveling expenses to the United States.

Harlow Shapley, the director of the Harvard
College Observatory, invited Payne to become a student in the newly formed astronomy program. Her
research was about stellar atmospheres and was published in 1925 when she was twenty-five years old.
She determined that the sun was made of mostly
hydrogen, contrary to current theory of that time. It
was the first dissertation in astronomy completed at
the observatory. She determined that the classification of stars developed by Annie Cannon was
directly related to the temperature of the stars.

In 1934 Payne married Sergei Gaposchkin, who also
was an astronomer. Together they raised three
children while continuing their work in astronomy.

Cecilia Payne-Gaposchkin saw herself as a field naturalist. She was the first woman to become a full professor at Harvard University, in 1956.

Payne-Gaposchkin was one of the first women to combine marriage, motherhood, and a scientific career.[14]

Payne and her husband worked together on many projects. They studied all the known variable stars brighter than tenth magnitude. The magnitude scale is a method used to describe how bright a star appears. Variable stars are stars that change their brightness in regular patterns.

Payne-Gaposchkin saw herself as a field naturalist with a knack for "bringing together facts that were previously unrelated and seeing a pattern in them."[15] She became the first woman at Harvard to become a full professor in 1956. She also was the first woman at Harvard to become the head of a department.

Payne-Gaposchkin wrote many articles and many books on astronomy. Most of her work focused on the properties of the Milky Way and the Magellanic Clouds. The Milky Way is the galaxy in which Earth belongs. The Magellanic Clouds are two small galaxies visible from the southern hemisphere.

Payne-Gaposchkin died in 1979. In her obituary notice, Elske V. P. Smith wrote:

> Students and colleagues will remember her for her prodigious memory. . . . Her knowledge was encyclopedic, her enthusiasm unbounded.[16]

Vera Rubin

9

Vera Rubin
(1928–   )

Vera Cooper was born in 1928. Her interest in astronomy began when she was a young girl in Washington, D.C. From her bedroom window she watched the constellations as they slowly traveled across the night sky. She says that when she was ten or twelve she found watching "the sky more interesting than sleeping."[1] She knew then that she wanted to be an astronomer.[2] The sky had created in her a strong desire to study the stars. Vera's mother and father encouraged her interest in science and in astronomy. When she was fourteen, her father, an electrical engineer, helped her build her first telescope from a lens and a cardboard linoleum tube. He also went with her to meetings of the local amateur astronomy club.[3]

Later as a high school student, she recalls one of her science teachers telling her not to pursue a career in science because science was no place for a girl.[4] However, this advice did not deter her, and she continued her interest in science and astronomy at Vassar College. In the mid-1900s, there were very few colleges that allowed women to study astronomy. Vera chose Vassar because she knew she would be able to follow her dream there. Maria Mitchell, one of Rubin's heroines, and one of the first American women astronomers, had taught at Vassar when it opened its doors in 1865.[5] Vera graduated from Vassar Female College in 1948.

After Vassar, Vera married Robert Rubin and went with her husband to Cornell University, where he was studying physics. She was unable to go to graduate school at Princeton University because they did not accept women into the astronomy program. Instead she entered Cornell as a graduate student. While she was a student there, Rubin chose to explore the large scale motions of the galaxies. A galaxy is a collection of billions of stars moving around a point in the center of the collection. The speeds of moving galaxies are very difficult to measure.

Rubin had to use data recorded by other astronomers because it was almost impossible for "normal" people to use the large telescopes. Rubin noticed that in addition to the outward motion of galaxies caused by the expansion of the universe, there was also some sideways motion. Rubin presented her findings at a meeting of the American Astronomical Society in 1950. She says, "It got an enormous amount of publicity, almost all negative, but at least, from then on, astronomers knew who I was."[6] The paper was rejected for publication by both the *Astronomical Journal* and the *Astrophysical Journal.* It seemed clear that most astronomers were unwilling to consider her work seriously. Rubin's four children were born between 1950 and 1960. The family returned to Washington, D.C., when Rubin's husband began his new job at the Applied Physics Lab. Frustrated with housework, Rubin longed to return to her studies.[7] She entered Georgetown University and continued her study of astronomy.

At Georgetown Rubin pursued her interest in galaxies. She focused her research on the distribution of galaxies. She wanted to know if the galaxies were randomly distributed across the sky or if they formed some kind of pattern. Computers were not easily available or widespread in the 1950s, so Rubin did most of the calculations on a desktop calculator. The calculations that would take a modern computer only a few minutes to complete took Rubin months and months to finish.

The assumption at the time by the community of astronomers was that the galaxies were evenly distributed throughout space. Rubin concluded, however, that the distribution of galaxies in the universe did not appear uniformly random, but rather that they seemed to be clumped together in groups. In 1954 when Rubin presented her findings, not many other astronomers seemed interested. When the topic was studied again in the late 1960s, it was discovered that many local galaxies seem to be going toward the constellations of Hydra and Centuaras. This phenomenon is now called the Rubin-Ford effect.[8]

In 1963 Rubin worked with Margaret and Geoffrey Burbidge in San Diego, California, and gained more confidence in herself as an astronomer. She says, "That was probably the most influential year in my life. In my mind I had at last become an astronomer, for the Burbidges were actually interested in my ideas."[9]

Until 1965 women were not permitted to use the telescopes at Mount Palomar Observatory. Rubin changed all that when she became the first woman ever to use the famous telescopes.

When Rubin returned to Washington, she joined the research staff at the Department of Terrestrial Magnetism. Working with W. Kent Ford, who had designed a way to collect light ten times faster than had been done before, Rubin returned to the questions that had intrigued her when she was studying at Cornell. "Do galaxies just go along for the ride as the universe flies outward, or do they move around on their own as well?" For the second time Rubin and Ford's results showed extra motion. This extra motion of galaxies seems to be caused by local currents that are separate from the motion caused by the general expansion.

Vera Rubin was a member of the research staff at the Department of Terrestrial Magnetism, in Washington, D.C.

Rubin's next area of research was on the rotation of spiral galaxies. A spiral galaxy is a flattened, rotating galaxy with pinwheel type arms. She was trying to determine why different spiral galaxies differ in brightness and structure. Some galaxies appear to be tightly wound with their arms close into the center. Some galaxies appear to be loosely wound with their arms spread wide. She thought that learning about the spin of a galaxy might help explain its particular shape. There was very little data available so Rubin began measuring the spinning rates of the Andromeda galaxy, a near neighbor to our Milky Way galaxy.

Rubin and Ford measured how fast the stars and gas in that galaxy were spinning around the center. They took measurements at different points on the galaxy from the center of the galaxy to the outer edge of the galaxy. When the data were analyzed, Rubin discovered that the galaxy did not rotate as she and the others were expecting. Astronomers had assumed that most of the mass of a galaxy would be concentrated in the center of the galaxy. This assumption meant that the stars and gas near the center of the galaxy would go around the center faster than the stars and gas near the edge. However, what Rubin and Ford found was that the stars and gas near the disk's edge also went around the center very fast, much faster than anyone had predicted.[10] The astronomers could not explain why the stars did not fly off the edge when the galaxy was spinning so quickly. Something must be holding the stars together. Rubin decided that that "something" must be a huge amount of material hidden somewhere in the galaxy and was not visible to her telescope.[11] This invisible material is called "dark matter." Astronomers now believe that there is more dark matter than visible matter in a galaxy and in the universe. However, there is no agreement about the nature of dark matter.

Rubin also discovered another interesting galaxy. It was a galaxy with half of the stars going around the center in one direction and the rest of the stars going around in the other direction.

One of Rubin's greatest contributions to science is that she likes to ask questions that have not been asked before. She says, "I must just like doing things that other people are not doing."[12] She also claims that she likes to stay out of controversy. However, the questions she asks and the type of research she does seem to lead her to the middle of intense astronomical debates about the nature of the universe.

Rubin says, "My work is extremely exciting. It is a joyous way to live. I cannot wait to get to work."[13] Rubin's work has changed the way astronomers look at the universe.

In 1993 Rubin was awarded the National Medal of Science by President Bill Clinton:

> For her pioneering research programs in observational cosmology which demonstrated that much of the matter in the universe is dark and for significant contributions to the realization that the universe is more complex and more mysterious than had been imagined.[14]

Carl Sagan

Carl Sagan
(1934–   )

Carl Sagan was born on November 9, 1934, in Brooklyn, New York. His father, a garment cutter, had been born in Russia. His early childhood was typical for a poor boy in the city. Sagan, however, was not typical. At a very early age he was already interested in the stars. He wanted to know more about them. When he went to the library, he recalls that he asked the librarian for a book on stars. The librarian gave him a book on movie stars. After some discussion, the librarian showed Carl the astronomy section of the library where he read everything that he could about stars. He discovered from his reading that the universe was larger than he could imagine.[1]

He also learned that the sun was a star and that planets went around the sun. At eight years old he had already decided that if planets went around one star, namely our sun, then planets must also go around other stars. There could be millions of planets because there were millions of stars.[2]

When Sagan was ten years old, he was introduced to science-fiction books. Most of the books he read were written by Edgar Burroughs. The setting for most of these stories was the planet Mars, named in the book as Barsoom.[3] Next he discovered a science-fiction magazine called *Astounding Science Fiction.* He liked the science in the magazine much better. Reading science fiction had an incredible influence on his thinking, causing many questions to enter his mind. He became curious about the possibility of intelligent life elsewhere in the universe.[4]

In 1951, when he was sixteen, he entered the University of Chicago. During his college career, he met and worked with many distinguished scientists. One was H.J. Muller of Indiana University, a Nobel prizewinner in biology, who was studying the origins of life. During the summer of his freshman year, Sagan worked for Muller in a biology laboratory in Indiana. This was his first real scientific work. Muller told Sagan to study chemistry and biology as well as astronomy if he wanted to continue research about life on other worlds.[5]

Sagan was beginning to make an impression on the faculty of the university, and he was becoming known on campus. He helped organize a campus lecture series on science because he wanted to bring science to the people. Many students other than science majors attended these lectures, some of which Sagan gave himself. Some of the science faculty were skeptical of his goals. They were not concerned about getting the general public interested in science. This was Sagan's first attempt to popularize science that ultimately led him to become one of the best-known scientists in the world. He is not well-known for any great discoveries or new theories, but he is known world-wide as one who takes complex scientific concepts and explains them in a way that the average person can understand.

Sagan went on to earn graduate degrees in physics and astronomy from the University of Chicago. He studied with Gerard Kuiper, a planetary astronomer, who also was interested in whether life could exist on other planets.

In 1959 the National Academy of Sciences set up a special committee to study possible ways of searching for life in space. Because of Sagan's interests in both biology and astronomy, Joshua Lederberg, a Nobel prizewinner in biology, suggested that Sagan be asked to serve on the committee.[6]

The community of scientists had been reluctant to discuss life in space. Many remembered the days of Percival Lowell and the embarrassing failure of his determination to find life on Mars. For years scientists avoided the issue, not wanting to be identified with what might be considered science-fiction thinking rather than real science. The formation of this new committee by the National Academy of Sciences lifted the stigma left by the Martian controversy that had occurred as a result of Lowell's observations of Mars. The search for life in the universe changed back from science fiction to real science.

Sagan has been on the forefront of this change. He says, "Studying alien life-forms is the only way to develop a broad understanding of biology. . . ."[7] While many scientists now see the search for other kinds of life in the universe as a respectable field of study, Sagan has become famous as a result of his interest and research in this area.

During the time of the Apollo moon landings, Sagan suggested that there might be some form of life, however microscopic, on the moon. Even if the life were the tiniest microbe, it might be possible for the astronauts to unknowingly bring it back to Earth. Sagan's suggestions were taken seriously by NASA and all material brought back from the moon was put in quarantine.[8] Sagan was committed to keeping this planet and all the planets uncontaminated.[9]

In 1966 Sagan and a Soviet scientist, I. S. Shklovskii, wrote a book together entitled *Intelligent Life in the Universe*. The book was not a science book as much as it was a book about science that people who were not scientists could understand. This book again raised the possibility of intelligent life somewhere in the universe. This joint effort showed that cooperation and collaboration were possible between the United States and the Soviet Union.[10]

When the *Pioneer 10* spacecraft was being designed for planetary exploration in the early 1970s, it occurred to Sagan that this would be a perfect opportunity to try to communicate with other intelligent life in the universe. *Pioneer 10* was scheduled to fly near the surface of Jupiter and some of the outer planets. The spacecraft was not intended to return to Earth, but was to continue its journey into the universe forever. The possibilities here were too great for Sagan to ignore. He contacted NASA and suggested that some type of message be sent along with the spacecraft. Much to Sagan's surprise and delight, NASA agreed to attach a small plaque to the spacecraft.

But how does one communicate with some unknown form of intelligence? What do you say? Sagan and his colleagues assumed that if some life form were intelligent enough to collect the spacecraft from space, they were probably intelligent enough to figure out the code.

One of the most difficult decisions to make was trying to show the Earth's location in the galaxy with some kind of diagram. The plaque contains some scientific information, as well as the drawings of a male and a female human being. The plaque is only six inches by nine inches in

Carl Sagan hopes to communicate with intelligent life in the universe. Here, Sagan stands near the Viking Mars Lander in the Mojave Desert.

size, but will be readable for hundreds of millions of years as it travels through space.[11]

Sagan was also responsible for helping plan other types of messages for later *Pioneer* and *Voyager* flights. One includes greetings in sixty human languages as well as greetings from humpback whales, pictures of humans from all over the world, and music from many cultures.[12]

Sagan is a prolific writer of both fiction and nonfiction. He writes about "real" science as well as science fiction. He is probably best known for his television series called *Cosmos.* This series, seen by millions of people around the world, tells the story of science and scientific explorations. Through this series, his many books, and his regular articles in *Parade Magazine,* Sagan has made the words of science household words. He has always believed that it is in the interest of science that as many people as possible know what is happening in the scientific community. Science should not be just for the scientists in their laboratories, but science should be for everyone.[13] He says, ". . . This is a democracy, and for us to make sure that the powers of science and technology are used properly and prudently, we ourselves must understand science and technology. . . . [14]

Sagan is David Duncan Professor of Astronomy and Space Science at Cornell University in Ithaca, New York.

Chapter Notes

Preface

1. Alan Lightman and Roberta Brawer, *ORIGINS: The Lives and Worlds of Modern Cosmologists* (Cambridge, Mass.: Harvard University Press, 1990), p. 302.

2. Daniel Cohen, *Carl Sagan: Superstar Scientist* (New York: Dodd, Mead & Company, 1987), p. 118.

Chapter 1

1. Phebe Mitchell Kendall, *Maria Mitchell: Life, Letters, and Journals* (Boston: Lee & Shepard Publishers, 1896), p. 8.

2. Helen Wright, *Sweeper of the Sky: The Life of Maria Mitchell, First Woman Astronomer in America* (New York: The Macmillan Company, 1949), pp. 13–16.

3. Kendall, p. 19.

4. Wright, p. 21.

5. Ibid., pp. 21–22.

6. Ibid., pp. 33–34.

7. Ibid., pp. 44–45.

8. Ibid., p. 61.

9. Ibid., p. 62.

10. Kendall, p. 235.

11. Peggy Aldrich Kidwell, "Three Women of American Astronomy," *American Scientist*, Vol. 78, No. 3 (May/June 1990), p. 246.

Chapter 2

1. A. Lawrence Lowell, *Biography of Percival Lowell* (New York: The Macmillan Company, 1935), p. 5.

2. Erik Berg, "Martians," *Astronomy* (September 1991), p. 15.

3. Lowell, p. 8.

4. Ibid., p. 60.

5. Bessie Zaban Jones and Lyle Gifford Boyd, *The Harvard College Observatory: The First Four Directorships, 1839–1919* (Cambridge, Mass.: Harvard University Press, 1971), p. 326.

6. Lowell, p. 64.

7. Ibid., p. 66.

8. Ibid.

9. Ibid., p. 77.

10. Ibid., p. 89.

11. William Graves Hoyt, *Lowell and Mars* (Tucson, Ariz.: The University of Arizona Press, 1976), p. 13.

12. Ibid., p. 280.

Chapter 3

1. Joseph L. Spradley, "The Industrious Mrs. Fleming," *Astronomy* (July 1990), p. 50.

2. Ibid., p. 48.

3. Annie J. Cannon, "Minor Contributions and Notes: Williamina Paton Fleming," *Astrophysical Journal,* Vol. 34 (1911), p. 314.

4. Spradley, p. 50.

5. Ibid.

6. Ibid.

7. Bessie Zaban Jones and Lyle Gifford Boyd, *The Harvard College Observatory: The First Four Directorships, 1839–1919* (Cambridge, Mass.: Harvard University Press, 1971), pp. 354–355.

8. Ibid., p. 394.

9. Cannon, pp. 316–317.

10. Ibid., p. 315.

11. Jones and Boyd, pp. 394–395.

Chapter 4

1. Edna Yost, *American Women of Science* (New York: Frederick A. Stokes Company, 1943), p. 30.

2. Ibid., p. 32.

3. Barbara Welther, "Annie Jump Cannon: Classifier of the Stars," *Mercury, The Journal of the Astronomical Society of the Pacific*, Vol. XIII, No. 1 (January/February 1984), p. 28.

4. Ibid., p. 29.

5. Paul Merrill, "Obituary Notices," *Royal Astronomical Society*, Vol. 102, No. 2 (1942), p. 76.

6. Vera Rubin, "Women's Work," *Science* (July/August 1986), p. 64.

7. Yost, p. 41.

9. Harlow Shapley, *Through Rugged Ways to the Stars* (New York: Charles Scribner's Sons, 1969), p. 92.

10. Merrill, p. 76.

11. "Report of the Committee to Visit the Astronomical Observatory of Harvard College," *Popular Astronomy*, Vol. 20 (1912), p. 684.

Chapter 5

1. Helen Wright, Joan N. Warnow and Charles Weiner, eds., *The Legacy of George Ellery Hale, Evolution of Astronomy and Scientific Institutions, in Pictures and Documents* (Cambridge, Mass.: The Massachusetts Institute of Technology, 1972), p. 2.

2. Ibid.

3. Ibid.

4. Donald E. Osterbrock, *Pauper & Prince, Ritchey, Hale, & Big American Telescopes* (Tucson, Ariz.: The University of Arizona Press, 1993), pp. 19–20.

5. Wright, p. 9.

6. Ibid., p. 22.

7. Ibid., p. 18.

8. Ibid., p. 19.

9. Ibid., p. 21.

10. William J. McPeak, "Building the Glass Giant of Palomar," *Astronomy* (December 1992), p. 32.

Chapter 6

1. Harlow Shapley, *Through Rugged Ways to the Stars* (New York: Charles Scribner's Sons, 1969), p. 13.

2. Ibid., p. 39.

3. Colin Wilson, *Starseekers* (Garden City, N.Y.: Doubleday & Company, Inc., 1980), pp. 232–233.

4. Helen Sawyer Hogg, "Shapley's Era", *The Harlow-Shapley Symposium on Globular Cluster Systems in Galaxies* (Boston: Kluwer Academic Publishers, 1988), p. 20–21.

Chapter 7

1. Donald Osterbrock, Joel A. Gwinn and Ronald S. Brashear, "Edwin Hubble and the Expanding Universe," *Scientific American*, Vol. 269, No. 1 (July 1993), p. 84.

2. Donald Osterbrock, Ronald S. Brashear and Joel A. Gwinn, "Self-made Cosmologist: The Education of Edwin Hubble," *Evolution of the Universe of Galaxies, Edwin Hubble Centennial Symposium*, ed. Richard G. Kron (San Francisco: Astronomical Society of the Pacific, 1990), pp. 6–7.

3. Hale to Hubble, June 9, 1919, Hale Microfilm.

4. Osterbrock, p. 12.

5. Robert W. Smith, "Edwin P. Hubble and the Transformation of Cosmology," *Physics Today*, Vol 43, No. 4 (April 1990), p. 55.

6. Norriss S. Hetherington, "Edwin Hubble's Cosmology," *Evolution of the Universe of Galaxies, Edwin Hubble Centennial Symposium*, ed. Richard G. Kron (San Francisco: Astronomical Society of the Pacific, 1990), p. 24.

Chapter 8

1. Peggy A. Kidwell, "Cecilia Payne-Gaposchkin: Astronomy in the Family," *Uneasy Careers and Intimate Lives: Women in Science 1789–1979*, ed. Pnina G. Abir-Am and Dorinda Outram (New Brunswick, N.J.: Rutgers University Press, 1987), pp. 219–220.

2. Cecilia Payne-Gaposchkin, *Cecilia Payne-Gaposchkin: An Autobiography and Other Recollections*, ed. Katherine Haramundanis (Cambridge, Mass.: Cambridge University Press, 1984), p. 97.

3. Ibid., p. 98.

4. Ibid.

5. Ibid., p. 99.

6. Ibid., p. 101.

7. Ibid.

8. Ibid., p. 102.

9. Ibid.

10. Ibid.

11. Ibid., p. 108.

12. Ibid., pp. 108–109.

13. Ibid.

14. Kidwell, p. 217.

15. Charles A. Whitney, "Cecilia Payne-Gaposchkin: An Astronomer's Astronomer," *Sky and Telescope,* Vol. 59, No. 3 (March 1980), p. 214.

16. Elske Smith, "Cecilia Payne-Gaposchkin," *Physics Today* (June 1980), p. 65.

Chapter 9

1. Barbara Sprungman and Leonard David, "Spiraling Among the Stars," *Odyssey* (March 1994), pp. 35–39.

2. Ibid.

3. Alan Lightman and Roberta Brawer, *ORIGINS: The Lives and Worlds of Modern Cosmologists* (Cambridge, Mass.: Harvard University Press, 1990), pp. 286–287.

4. Sally Stevens, "Women in Astronomy," A Slide Information Set, The Astronomical Society of the Pacific, 1992, p. 33.

5. Helen Wright, *Sweeper in the Sky: The Life of Maria Mitchell, First Woman Astronomer in America* (New York: The Macmillan Company, 1949), pp. 146–149.

6. Marcia Bartusiak, "The Woman Who Spins the Stars," *Discover,* Vol. 11, No. 10 (October 1990), p. 90.

7. Ibid.

8. Stevens, p. 33.

9. Bartusiak, p. 91.

10. Ibid.

11. Ibid.

12. Lightman, p. 296.

13. Alice Fins, *Women in Science* (Skokie, Ill.: National Textbook Co., 1979), p. 65.

14. Barbara Mandula and Resha Putzrath, "AWIS Members Awarded Medal of Science," *AWIS Magazine* (January/February 1994), p. 12.

Chapter 10

1. Carl Sagan, "Wonder and Skepticism," *Skeptical Inquirer* (January/February 1995), pp. 24–25.

2. Daniel Cohen, *Carl Sagan: Superstar Scientist* (New York: Dodd, Mead & Company, 1987), p. 12.

3. Ibid., p. 13.

4. Ibid., pp. 13–15.

5. Ibid., pp. 18–20.

6. Ibid., pp. 23–24.

7. Ibid., p. 31.

8. Ibid., p. 33.

9. Ibid., p. 34.

10. Ibid., pp. 38–39.

11. Ibid., p. 44.

12. Ibid., p. 49.

13. Robert Resnick, "1990 Oersted Medal: Carl Sagan," *The Physics Teacher*, Vol. 28 (March 1990), p. 138.

14. Sagan, p. 26.

Index

About the Author

Carole Ann Camp teaches courses in elementary and secondary science education. Besides writing for young people, she frequently visits the many stone circles in Great Britain. Dr. Camp lives with her husband, Charles, and is the mother of two grown children, Morgan and Heather.